D1597008

The Chowder Trail
COOKBOOK

The best recipes for an East Coast specialty

ELAINE ELLIOT AND VIRGINIA LEE

FORMAC PUBLISHING COMPANY LIMITED
HALIFAX

Formac Publishing Company Limited recognizes the support of the
Province of Nova Scotia through the Department of Communities,
Culture and Heritage. We are pleased to work in partnership with the
Province of Nova Scotia to develop and promote our cultural resources
for all Nova Scotians. We acknowledge the support of the Canada
Council for the Arts, which last year invested $153 million to bring the
arts to Canadians throughout the country. This project has been made
possible in part by the Government of Canada.

Cover design by Tyler Cleroux

Library and Archives Canada Cataloguing in Publication

Title: The chowder trail cookbook : the best recipes for an East Coast
    specialty / Elaine Elliot and Virginia Lee.
Names: Elliot, Elaine, 1939- author. | Lee, Virginia, 1947- author.
Description: Includes index.
Identifiers: Canadiana 20200158791 | ISBN 9781459506091
    (hardcover)
Subjects: LCSH: Soups—Nova Scotia. | LCSH: Cooking, Canadian—
    Maritime Provinces style. | LCGFT: Cookbooks.
Classification: LCC TX757 .E455 2020 | DDC 641.81/3—dc23

Formac Publishing Company Limited
5502 Atlantic Street
Halifax, Nova Scotia, Canada
B3H 1G4
www.formac.ca

Printed and bound in Korea.

CONTENTS

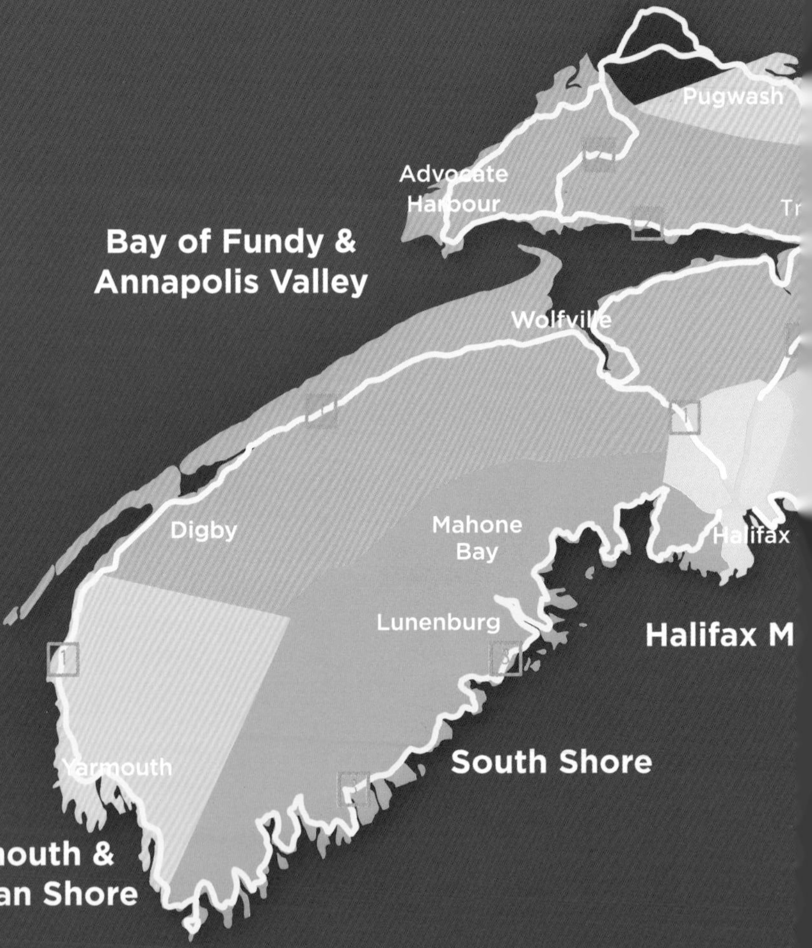

Pugwash

Advocate
Harbour

Tr

**Bay of Fundy &
Annapolis Valley**

Wolfville

Digby

Mahone
Bay

Halifax

Lunenburg

Halifax M

1

South Shore

Yarmouth

**Yarmouth &
Acadian Shore**

Ingonish

Cape Breton
Island

Inverness

Baddeck

Sydney

Louisbourg

Northumberland
Shore

Port
Hawkesbury

Antigonish

ou

Guysborough

Eastern Shore

■ Halifax Metro
■ South Shore
■ Eastern Shore
■ Cape Breton Island
▨ Yarmouth & Acadian Shore
▨ Bay of Fundy & Annapolis Valley
▨ Northumberland Shore

INTRODUCTION

Living in a province almost entirely surrounded by the sea, it is understandable that soups made with fresh seafood are a staple of many Nova Scotian diets. We were delighted when so many chefs offered to share their secret recipes — and now you can make these delicious, healthy chowders in your own kitchen.

Many of the chefs emphasize the utilization of fresh, sustainable seafood and locally grown vegetables. Where else but in Nova Scotia will you find such an abundance of seafood? Plump scallops, lobster, haddock, halibut, mussels and salmon are a few of our local species. Little wonder that almost every restaurant or café offers chowder on their menu. To our surprise, we found unique differences in each of the recipes, with each chef adding his or her own personal touch.

Most restaurants prepare their own fish stock or broth in large quantities, and a few have shared recipes for its preparation. However, since it may not be convenient for you to prepare broths from scratch, there are several good products that can be added to water: Minor's Seafood Base or Better than Bouillon in paste form, and Knorr Seafood cubes or powder. Simply follow the directions on the package and you have a flavourful base for a great chowder.

We hope you enjoy trying these recipes in your own kitchen and we encourage you to visit the establishments that supplied them. Bon Appétit!

Elaine Elliot and Virginia Lee

SMOKED YUKON GOLD POTATO CHOWDER

CHIVES CANADIAN BISTRO, HALIFAX, NS

So simple. So good. Make the base in advance, then simply add whatever fresh seafood you can find — even if you only use haddock, this chowder is delicious and satisfying.

1 cup maple, apple or hickory wood chips
2 pounds cooked Yukon Gold potatoes, peeled and quartered
¼ cup butter
1 cup diced onion
1 cup sliced leek (white parts only)
½ cup chopped celery
3 cloves garlic
2 teaspoons white pepper
1 teaspoon salt
½ cup white wine
6 cups chicken stock
2 cups milk
1 ½ cups heavy cream (35% m.f.)
2 to 3 pounds mixed fresh seafood, cut in bite-size chunks

Set barbecue to high. In disposable foil pan, evenly spread wood chips and lightly sprinkle with water. Place pan on hot grill, close lid and grill until beginning to smoke, 10 to 14 minutes. In another pan, evenly arrange potatoes; place on grill, close lid and smoke for 5 to 7 minutes. Remove and set aside. Remove and discard wood chips.

In stockpot over medium-high heat, melt butter; sauté onion, leek, celery, garlic, pepper and salt until onion is translucent. Stir in wine and cook, stirring to deglaze pan, until liquid has reduced by half. Reduce heat, stir in reserved potatoes, stock and milk; simmer for 30 to 45 minutes. In small batches in blender, purée. Strain into large saucepan.

Gently stir in cream and seafood. Bring to a simmer; cook just until chowder is hot and fish is cooked. Serve with Chives Buttermilk Biscuits, page 86.

Serves 6 to 8.

Cooking tip
Use haddock or other seafood — such as lobster, scallops, mussels, Atlantic cold-water shrimp, canned baby clams, halibut or even salmon.

NOVA SCOTIA SEAFOOD CHOWDER

EMMA'S EATERY,
EASTERN PASSAGE, NS

True to the tradition on the Eastern Shore, Chef Kim Stacey prefers steaming instead of boiling fresh lobster to preserve the sweetness of the meat rather than losing it to the cooking water. And for the best flavour, she says, serve scallops medium-rare.

1 lobster (about 1 ½ pounds)
¼ cup butter
1 cup chopped carrot
1 cup chopped celery
1 cup chopped onion
1 sprig fresh thyme (¼ teaspoon dried)
¼ teaspoon summer savory
2 tablespoons white wine
2 cups fish stock
2 potatoes, cut in small cubes
1 cup heavy cream (35% m.f.)
1 pound haddock, cubed
½ pound large scallops
Sea salt and pepper to taste

Into large stockpot, pour 2 inches salt water (or fresh water with 1 tablespoon salt); bring to a boil. Add lobster, cover tightly and steam until cooked, 8 to 10 minutes. Drain, set aside and let cool enough to handle. Keeping claws whole and cutting tail into pieces, remove meat from shells. Discarding shells, set aside.

In large pot over medium-high heat, melt butter; sauté carrot, celery and onion for 2 to 3 minutes. Stir in thyme and savory; sauté until carrot is tender and onion is translucent.

Stir in wine and cook, stirring to deglaze pan, for 1 minute. Remove and discard thyme. Stir in fish stock and bring to a boil. Add potatoes; simmer until softened, about 5 minutes. Stir in cream.

Reduce heat to medium and add haddock and scallops; simmer just until cooked, 4 to 5 minutes. Remove from heat; stir in reserved lobster. Season to taste with salt and pepper.

Serves 4.

FIVE FISH SEAFOOD CHOWDER

THE FIVE FISHERMEN RESTAURANT & GRILL, HALIFAX, NS

Across the province, chowder styles vary — some are thickened, while others are an uncomplicated combination of seafood and milk or cream. This chowder has a unique broth — accented with fresh vegetables, sherry and seasonings — and features five Atlantic seafood species.

1 pound Yukon Gold potatoes, cubed
8 tablespoons unsalted butter
8 tablespoons all-purpose flour
8 cups water
1 teaspoon Worcestershire sauce
2 dashes Tabasco sauce
2 tablespoons lemon juice
1 teaspoon salt
8 ounces shrimp
8 ounces scallops
4 ounces haddock, cubed
4 ounces salmon, cubed
2 tablespoons olive oil
2 carrots, diced
2 stalks celery, diced
1 sweet onion, diced
1 tablespoon dried summer savory
1 teaspoon dried dill
2 tablespoons sherry
8 ounces cooked lobster meat, cut in bite-size chunks
1 cup heavy cream (35% m.f.)
Salt and pepper to taste

In large pot of boiling salted water, cook potatoes until tender. Drain and set aside.

In small saucepan over medium heat, melt butter; add flour and cook, stirring constantly, for 2 minutes. Remove from heat and set aside.

In large saucepan, bring water, Worcestershire sauce, Tabasco sauce, lemon juice and salt to a boil; reduce heat to simmer. Gently stir in shrimp; poach for 2 minutes. With slotted spoon, transfer shrimp to bowl. Set aside. In batches, repeat process, to cook scallops, haddock and salmon. Set poaching liquid aside.

In large heavy saucepan or Dutch oven, heat oil over medium heat; sauté carrots, celery, onion, summer savory and dill until tender and golden, about 8 minutes. Increase heat to high, add sherry and cook, stirring to deglaze pan.

Add reserved poaching liquid and bring to a boil. One tablespoon at a time and stirring well after each addition, add flour mixture, adding only until broth is desired consistency. Stir in reserved potatoes and poached seafood, lobster and cream; cook until warmed through. Season to taste with salt and pepper.

Serves 4 to 6.

ACADIAN SEAFOOD CHOWDER

HARBOUR CITY BAR AND GRILL AT DELTA HALIFAX, HALIFAX, NS

Chef Camm has served variations of this recipe for more than 25 years. Depending on the location of his current kitchen and the day's catch, he adds or subtracts seafood ingredients. He encourages home cooks to do the same, and to experiment with other herbs and wines to change the flavour. As he says, "Be creative and make it your own!"

2 cups cubed potatoes
4 slices bacon, cut in ½–inch pieces
1 onion, finely chopped
¼ cup diced celery
2 ½ tablespoons unsalted butter
2 tablespoons diced sweet red pepper
2 ½ tablespoons all-purpose flour
4 cups fish stock
2 cups milk (2% m.f.)
1 cup heavy cream (35% m.f.)
2 tablespoons Pernod liqueur
3 sprigs fresh thyme (1 ½ teaspoons dried)
4 ounces bay scallops
4 ounces small shrimp
4 ounces haddock, cut in bite-size pieces
4 ounces salmon, cut in bite-size pieces
½ pound lobster meat, cut in bite-size pieces
Salt and pepper to taste

In large pot of boiling salted water, cook potatoes just until tender. Drain and set aside.

In large saucepan over medium heat, cook bacon halfway. Stir in onion, celery, butter and red pepper; sauté until onion is translucent.

Add flour; cook, stirring constantly, for 2 minutes. Slowly add fish stock, milk and cream, stirring. Stir in reserved potatoes, Pernod and thyme; bring to a low simmer.

Stir in scallops, shrimp, haddock and salmon and return to simmer; cook until fish flakes easily with fork. Gently stir in lobster meat; cook until heated through. Season to taste with salt and pepper.

Serves 6.

17

SUSTAINABLE SEAFOOD CHOWDER

MORRIS EAST RESTAURANT & WINE BAR, HALIFAX AND BEDFORD, NS

A favourite with both customers and staff, this recipe combines sustainable seafood and fresh-off-the-farm produce. The corn and jalapeños add crunch and kick!

2 cups cubed Yukon Gold potatoes

¼ cup butter

2 carrots, diced

2 celery stalks, diced

2 jalapeño peppers, seeded and minced

1 cup chopped onion

1 ½ tablespoons minced garlic

¼ cup all-purpose flour

Mussel Broth (recipe follows)

2 cups whole milk (3.5% m.f.)

2 cups heavy cream (35% m.f.)

Corn from 2 oven-roasted cobs (1 ½ cups frozen)

12 ounces salmon, cubed

12 ounces haddock, cubed

8 ounces scallops, halved if large

Reserved mussel meat from Mussel Broth (recipe follows)

2 tablespoons lemon juice

2 tablespoons chopped fresh tarragon (2 teaspoons dried)

2 tablespoons chopped parsley

Salt and pepper to taste

In large pot of boiling salted water, cook potatoes just until tender. Drain and set aside.

In large heavy saucepan or Dutch oven over medium-high heat, melt butter; sauté carrots, celery, jalapeños and onion until tender, about 6 minutes. Reduce heat to medium, stir in garlic and cook for 3 minutes.

Stir in flour; cook, stirring constantly, for 2 minutes. Increase heat to high and stir in Mussel Broth; cook, stirring to deglaze pan. Gently stir in reserved potatoes, milk, cream and corn. Reduce heat and bring to a low simmer; cook, stirring occasionally, for 10 minutes.

Gently stir in salmon, haddock and scallops; cook over medium heat until fish flakes easily with fork, about 5 minutes. Gently stir in reserved mussel meat, lemon juice, tarragon and parsley; cook until heated through. Season to taste with salt and pepper.

Serves 6.

MUSSEL BROTH

2 ½ pounds mussels
2 teaspoons butter
1 carrot, diced
1 stalk celery, diced
½ cup diced white onion
2 tablespoons minced garlic
3 tablespoons white wine

Under cold running water, scrub and de-beard mussels, discarding any that are damaged or don't close when lightly tapped. Set aside.

In large saucepan over medium-high heat, melt butter; sauté carrot, celery, onion and garlic until tender, about 6 minutes. Increase heat to high, add wine and cook, stirring to deglaze pan. Stir in reserved mussels; cover and cook until mussels open, about 5 minutes.

Strain broth into bowl and set aside. Remove and discard any unopened mussels. Discarding shells, remove meat and set aside.

SEAFOOD CHOWDER

SAEGE BISTRO,
HALIFAX, NS

This substantial chowder is loaded with clams, scallops, shrimp and chunks of haddock and salmon — all in a creamy base that's brightened with dill.

24 fresh mussels
5 cups fish stock, divided
2 cups cubed potatoes
1 carrot, diced
10 tablespoons butter, divided
1 ½ stalks celery, chopped
½ Spanish onion, chopped
8 tablespoons rice flour
2 cups heavy cream (35% m.f.)
2 tablespoons chopped fresh dill
½ pound cold-water shrimp
½ pound scallops
4 ounces haddock, cubed
4 ounces salmon, cubed
½ cup shucked fresh clams, with juice
½ leek (white and light green parts only), sliced
⅓ cup white wine
2 tablespoons cooking sherry
¼ teaspoon lemon pepper
Pinch of nutmeg
Pinch of cayenne pepper
Salt to taste

Under cold running water, scrub and de-beard mussels, discarding any that are damaged or don't close when lightly tapped. Set aside.

In saucepan over medium heat, bring 2 cups of the fish stock to a simmer; cook potatoes and carrot just until tender, about 5 minutes. Remove from heat and set aside.

In large heavy saucepan or Dutch oven over low heat, melt 7 tablespoons of the butter; sweat celery and onion until translucent, about 8 minutes. Stir in rice flour; cook, stirring constantly, for 1 minute. Slowly stir in remaining fish stock until blended and smooth.

Increase heat to medium, stir in cream and cook, stirring frequently, until thickened, about 3 minutes. Stir in dill and reserved potatoes, carrot and fish stock. Stir in shrimp, scallops, haddock, salmon and clams and juice; bring to a simmer and cook just until cooked through, about 6 minutes.

Meanwhile, in saucepan over low heat, melt remaining butter; sweat leek until bright green, about 5 minutes. Increase heat to high, add wine and sherry; cook, stirring to deglaze pan. Stir in reserved mussels, cover and cook until opened, about 5 minutes. Reserving cooking liquid, strain. Remove and discard any unopened mussels. Add mussels and reserved cooking liquid to simmering broth, along with lemon pepper, nutmeg and cayenne. Season to taste with salt.

Serves 6 to 8.

CURRY LOBSTER CHOWDER

SEASONS BY ATLANTICA, HALIFAX, NS

Tantalizing Indian spices and lime combine with fresh Nova Scotia lobster in this gluten-free soup. Chef Luis Clavel's chowder is a signature dish on the Seasons menu.

1 tablespoon vegetable oil
½ pound unpeeled sweet potato, diced
2 large cloves garlic, finely minced
2-inch piece ginger, finely minced
2 tablespoons diced white onion
2 teaspoons garam masala
1 ½ teaspoons curry powder
1 teaspoon ground coriander
½ teaspoon ground cumin
3 cups Lobster Stock (recipe follows)
2 ½ cups tomato juice
6 ounces fresh tomatoes, diced with seeds
¼ bunch fresh cilantro, chopped
2 teaspoons lime juice
Salt and pepper to taste
1 pound Boiled Atlantic Lobster meat (recipe follows), cut in bite-size pieces

In large saucepan over medium-high heat, warm oil; sauté sweet potato, garlic, ginger, onion, garam masala, curry, coriander and cumin until onion is translucent, about 5 minutes.

Stir in Lobster Stock and tomato juice; bring to a boil. Reduce heat, cover and simmer for 30 to 40 minutes. Stir in tomatoes, cilantro and lime juice; return to simmer. Season to taste with salt and pepper. Evenly divide Boiled Atlantic Lobster meat between 4 to 6 serving bowls; cover with chowder.

Serves 4 to 6.

BOILED ATLANTIC LOBSTER AND LOBSTER STOCK

4 quarts water
1 tablespoon each granulated sugar and salt
3 lobsters (each 1 ¼ pounds)
2 Spanish onions, cut in large chunks
1 celery root, cut in large chunks
1 large carrot, cut in large chunks
1 bunch fresh tarragon, chopped
1 bay leaf
2 cups white wine
2 tablespoons tomato paste

In large stockpot, combine water, sugar and salt and bring to a boil. One at a time and headfirst, immerse lobsters in boiling water; return to a boil, cover and cook until bright red, 10 to 12 minutes. Using tongs and reserving cooking liquid, remove lobsters and rinse under cold running water. Set aside and let cool enough to handle. Shell lobsters. Set meat aside.

Transfer shells to stockpot along with reserved cooking liquid. Stir in onions, celery root, carrot, tarragon, bay leaf, wine and tomato paste; bring to a boil. Reduce heat and bring to a simmer; cook, uncovered, for 45 minutes.

With slotted spoon, transfer large chunks to bowl. Through fine-mesh sieve lined with cheesecloth, strain remaining stock into clean pot.

Bring stock to a boil; cook until reduced by half. (If desired, transfer stock to airtight container and refrigerate for up to 4 days or freeze for up to 3 months.)

Yields 6 to 8 cups.

SOUTH
SHORE

CHARLOTTE LANE SEAFOOD CHOWDER

CHARLOTTE LANE CAFÉ & GIFT SHOP, SHELBURNE, NS

In this recipe, Chef Glauser merges inspirations and ideas from his professional experience and his sampling of homemade chowders from the Shelburne area. He takes the best features from each dish to create his own combination, and recommends that home cooks do that, too. He suggests that you start with his base recipe, then mix and match the ingredients: Replace regular potatoes with sweet potatoes. Add six ounces crumbled, cooked bacon. Season with chopped fresh tarragon or saffron threads. Substitute the fresh haddock with smoked haddock. Add lobster, clams or mussels. Omit the salt and season with finely chopped dried dulse and wakame.

2 tablespoons butter
2 tablespoons all-purpose flour
1 ½ cups heavy cream (35% m.f.)
²/₃ cups dry white wine
4 teaspoons Worcestershire sauce
2 cups cubed potatoes
½ cup finely chopped onion
1 pound each haddock, scallops and small shrimp
2 teaspoons fish-base seasoning
Salt and pepper to taste

In large saucepan over medium heat, melt butter; stir in flour and cook, stirring constantly, for 1 minute. Slowly add cream, whisking until blended and smooth. Stir in wine and Worcestershire sauce; reduce heat to low and cook, stirring occasionally, for 15 minutes.

In large pot of boiling salted water, cook potatoes and onion until tender; drain vegetables and stir into cream mixture.

In large saucepan of simmering salted water, cook haddock, scallops and shrimp until two-thirds cooked, 3 to 5 minutes (do not overcook). Reserving 2 cups of the poaching liquid, drain. Transfer haddock, scallops and shrimp to cream mixture; gently stir in.

Stir fish-base seasoning into reserved poaching liquid until combined; stir into cream mixture until desired consistency. Season to taste with salt and pepper.

Serves 6 to 8.

GRAND BANKER SEAFOOD CHOWDER

GRAND BANKER BAR & GRILL, LUNENBURG, NS

This distinctive chowder serves up a taste of the scallops and haddock that are characteristic of the Lunenburg fishery. In a pinch, hake, pollock, ling cod or any lean white-fleshed fish could be used in place of the haddock.

2 tablespoons butter
1 onion, finely diced
10 sprigs fresh thyme
2 bay leaves
2 potatoes, cubed
5 cups fish stock
1 ¼ pounds haddock, cut in 2-inch cubes
¾ pound scallops
1 can (10 ounce) baby clams, with juice
½ pound Atlantic cold-water shrimp
1 cup half-and-half cream (10% m.f.)
Salt and pepper to taste
Chopped parsley

In large saucepan over medium-high heat, melt butter; sauté onion until tender (do not allow to brown). Tie thyme and bay leaves into cheesecloth bundle and add to pan along with potatoes and stock; bring to a simmer and cook until potatoes are tender. Reduce heat to low, remove and discard bundle and stir in haddock and scallops; cook just until fish is cooked, about 5 minutes. Stir in clams and juice, shrimp and cream; cook until heated through. Season to taste with salt and pepper. Sprinkle each serving with parsley.

Serves 4 to 6.

⒫ Cooking tip

Made without a roux or thickener, this light chowder may be thinner than most chowders, but it boasts large chunks of fish and seafood.

LANE'S CREAMY SEAFOOD CHOWDER

LANE'S PRIVATEER INN, LIVERPOOL, NS

Evolving since the early 1960s, Lane's seafood chowder has been tweaked and enhanced by succeeding chefs in its kitchen. This collaborative recipe, however, has always been faithful to the fresh ingredients that let the seafood be the star. Not thickened with a roux, this chowder is ideal for anyone who is sensitive to gluten.

¼ to ⅓ cup butter, divided
1 yellow onion, diced
1 large potato, cubed
2 cups water
½ pound haddock fillet, in one piece
4 ounces scallops, halved if large
4 ounces cooked lobster, cut in bite-size pieces
2 green onions (white and light green parts only), chopped
2 tablespoons chopped fresh basil (2 teaspoons dried)
2 teaspoons chopped fresh tarragon (½ teaspoon dried)
2 cups coffee cream (18% m.f.)
Salt and pepper to taste

In heavy saucepan over low heat, melt 1 tablespoon of the butter; sweat onion until translucent, 10 to 12 minutes. Add potato and water and bring to a boil; reduce heat and simmer for 5 minutes. Lay haddock fillet over potatoes; simmer until potatoes are tender and fish flakes easily with fork, about 5 minutes. Set aside (do not drain).

In skillet over medium-high heat, melt remaining butter; sauté scallops, lobster, green onions, basil and tarragon until scallops are opaque, about 3 minutes. Transfer to potato mixture and stir in cream; cook until heated through. Season to taste with salt and pepper.

Serves 4.

MATEUS BISTRO
SOUTH SHORE CHOWDER

MATEUS BISTRO,
MAHONE BAY, NS

This gluten-free recipe calls for fresh haddock and mussels. Chef Matthew Krizen uses local seafood from nearby Indian Point, then adds an exotic taste of Eastern Europe — marjoram — to the broth.

1 ¾ pounds mussels, divided
6 cups water
Pinch salt
2 tablespoons vegetable oil
¾ cup sliced carrots
¾ cup chopped onion
2 tablespoons crumbled dried marjoram
1 unpeeled potato, cubed
3 cups heavy cream (35% m.f.)
1 pound haddock, cubed
Salt and pepper to taste
2 tablespoons chopped parsley

Under cold running water, scrub and de-beard mussels, discarding any that are damaged or don't close when lightly tapped. Set aside.

In large saucepan, combine water and salt; bring to a boil. Add 1 pound of the mussels; cover and cook until opened, about 3 minutes. Reserving cooking liquid, strain through fine-mesh sieve. Discard any unopened mussels. Set aside until cool enough to handle. Remove and discard shells. Set meat aside.

In large saucepan over medium heat, warm oil; sweat carrots and onion, stirring often, for 3 to 5 minutes (do not let brown). Stir in marjoram. Add reserved cooking liquid and bring to a boil. Reduce heat and simmer for 6 to 8 minutes. Stir in potato; simmer for about 10 minutes.

Stir in cream; cook until potatoes are tender. Gently stir in remaining whole mussels and haddock; cover and simmer until mussels have opened and fish flakes easily with fork, 4 to 5 minutes. Remove and discard any unopened mussels. Stir in reserved mussel meat. Season to taste with salt and pepper. Sprinkle each serving with parsley.

Serves 6 to 8.

South Shore

OLD FISH FACTORY SEAFOOD CHOWDER

THE OLD FISH FACTORY RESTAURANT & ICE HOUSE BAR, LUNENBURG, NS

If you wonder if your waistline can stretch to accommodate another bowl of thick and creamy chowder, try this version. It highlights haddock, baby shrimp, scallops and clams in a lightened-up milky broth.

2 cups cubed potatoes

4 cups water

3 teaspoons fish-base seasoning

½ teaspoon white pepper

½ teaspoon onion powder

1 onion, finely chopped

2 pounds haddock fillet, cubed

4 ounces scallops

2 cups whole milk (3.5% m.f.)

4 ounces cooked shrimp

1 can (10 ounce) baby clams, with juice

8 ounces lobster, cut in bite-size pieces

2 to 3 tablespoons butter

Salt to taste

Chopped parsley

In large pot of boiling salted water, cook potatoes just until tender. Drain and set aside.

In large saucepan, stir together water, fish-base seasoning, pepper and onion powder until seasoning has dissolved. Add onion and bring to a boil. Reduce heat to a simmer; gently stir in haddock and scallops; cook until fish flakes easily with fork, about 5 minutes. Stir in milk, shrimp, clams and juice and reserved potatoes; cook until heated through (do not let boil).

Gently stir in lobster and butter. Season to taste with salt and pepper (and additional onion powder, if desired). Sprinkle each serving with parsley.

Serves 4 to 6.

Cooking tip
If you're looking for a chowder that's lightened up, this one uses milk, not cream and is also gluten-free.

HEARTY SEAFOOD CHOWDER

QUARTERDECK GRILL, SUMMERVILLE CENTRE, NS

Chef John Dunbar uses French beurre manie or "handled butter" to thicken the broth. If you like, he says, you can use mussels or any other seafood in this soup.

⅓ cup butter, softened
⅓ cup all-purpose flour
1 tablespoon butter
1 small onion, finely diced
1 large clove garlic, minced
2 teaspoons finely chopped fresh rosemary
2 cups heavy cream (35% m.f.)
2 cups milk
2 cups water
2 teaspoons fish-base seasoning
¾ pound haddock, cut in bite-size pieces
¾ pound scallops
3 ounces cooked lobster meat
Salt and pepper to taste

In small bowl with fingers, blend ⅓ cup butter with flour, then press into ½-inch balls of roux. Set aside.

In large saucepan over medium-high heat, melt 1 tablespoon butter; sauté onion, garlic and rosemary until onion is translucent, about 6 minutes.

Meanwhile, in another saucepan, combine cream, milk, water and fish-base seasoning; bring to a simmer. One ball at a time, add roux, whisking after each addition to blend and adding until broth reaches desired consistency.

Stir broth into onion mixture; bring to a low simmer. Gently stir in haddock, scallops and lobster meat; cook until fish flakes easily with fork, 4 to 5 minutes. Season to taste with salt and pepper.

Serves 6.

Cooking tip
This recipe uses the French method of beurre manie or "handled butter" to thicken the chowder.

ROOT VEGETABLE SEAFOOD CHOWDER

RHUBARB RESTAURANT, INDIAN HARBOUR, NS

Chef Jon Geneau buys his lobster at Ryer Lobsters, located "just down the road." We'll guess that the root vegetables are also harvested nearby. His key ingredients are a generous helping of cream, fresh lemon juice and parsley.

6 quarts water
2 tablespoons salt
1 lobster (about 1 ½ pounds)
1 pound mussels
⅓ cup butter
1 cup diced Spanish onion
1 carrot, cubed
½ stalk celery, sliced
1 cup cubed potato
¼ cup cubed turnip
¼ cup cubed parsnip
4 to 6 ounces smoked Atlantic salmon, thinly sliced
½ pound haddock, cubed
1 cup heavy cream (35% m.f.)
2 tablespoons lemon juice
Salt and pepper to taste
½ cup chopped parsley

In large pot, combine water and salt; cook lobster for 12 minutes. With tongs, remove lobster and let cool enough to handle. Strain cooking liquid into bowl; set 3 cups aside. Discarding shells, remove lobster meat, break into bite-size pieces and set aside.

Under cold running water, scrub and de-beard mussels, discarding any that are damaged or do not close when lightly tapped. Set aside.

In large saucepan over medium heat, melt butter; sauté onion until translucent, about 5 minutes (do not let brown). Stir in carrot and celery; cook, stirring often, for 5 minutes. Stir in potato, turnip, parsnip and reserved cooking liquid; simmer until vegetables are tender.

Gently stir in salmon, haddock and reserved lobster and mussels; cover and simmer until mussels have opened and fish flakes easily with fork, 5 to 6 minutes. Remove and discard any unopened mussels. Gently stir in cream and lemon juice; cook until heated. Season to taste with salt and pepper. Sprinkle each serving with parsley.

Serves 4 to 6.

AWARD-WINNING SMOKED SEAFOOD CHOWDER

SALT SHAKER DELI, LUNENBURG, NS

Chef Salvador serves succulent scallops, steamed mussels and Atlantic shrimp in a chowder base flavoured with smoked haddock. You'll want to enjoy this one again and again.

2 pounds mussels
⅔ cup cold water
1 tablespoon vegetable oil
2 large potatoes, diced
1 large carrot, diced
1 onion, diced
8 ounces smoked haddock, shredded
2 cups heavy cream (35% m.f.)
2 cups milk (2% m.f.) or whole milk (3.5% m.f.)
3 to 4 tablespoons all-purpose flour
1 to 2 tablespoons butter
¾ pound large scallops
¼ pound cooked Atlantic cold-water shrimp
Salt and pepper, to taste
2 tablespoons finely chopped parsley

Under cold running water, scrub and de-beard mussels, discarding any that are damaged or don't close when lightly tapped. In large pot, bring water to a boil; steam mussels until opened, about 6 minutes. Remove and discard any unopened mussels. Set aside until cool enough to handle. Remove and discard shells. Set aside.

In heavy stockpot or Dutch oven over medium-low heat, warm oil; sauté potatoes, carrot, onion and haddock, stirring often, until vegetables are tender, 12 to 15 minutes. Stir in cream; bring to a simmer.

In small bowl, combine milk and flour; stir into broth and bring to a boil. Reduce heat and simmer until thick enough to coat the back of a spoon, about 5 minutes.

Meanwhile, rinse scallops, pat dry and remove any connector mussels. In skillet, melt butter then sear scallops until barely opaque, 1 to 2 minutes per side. Stir into broth along with shrimp; cook until heated through. Adjust seasoning with salt and pepper. Sprinkle each serving with parsley.

Serves 4.

Cooking tip

Affectionately known as "finnan haddie," the smoked haddock lends this dish a subtle richness.

BACON, CORN AND PRAWN CHOWDER

THE BISCUIT EATER CAFÉ & BOOKS, MAHONE BAY, NS

Bursting with flavour, this chowder is a change from the traditional cream-based variety common on the East Coast.

4 slices bacon, cut in ½-inch pieces
1 large carrot, diced
1 ½ celery stalks, diced
1 cup chopped sweet onion
2 tablespoons tomato paste
½ cup white wine
3 cups seafood, chicken or vegetable stock
2 large Yukon Gold potatoes, cubed
Corn from 4 cobs (or 4 cups frozen corn)
1 bay leaf
1 tablespoon granulated sugar
2 teaspoons dried basil (1 ½ tablespoon fresh, chopped)
1 ½ teaspoon dried oregano
1 cup heavy cream (35% m.f.)
2 teaspoons olive oil
2 to 3 teaspoons smoked paprika
1 teaspoon finely minced garlic
Dash salt and pepper
12 large prawns, peeled and deveined
Green onion, chopped

In large saucepan over medium-high heat, sauté bacon until crisp. Reduce heat to medium and stir in carrot, celery and onion; cook, stirring occasionally, until onion is translucent, about 5 minutes. Stir in tomato paste until combined.

Increase heat to high, add wine and cook, stirring to deglaze pan. Stir in stock along with potatoes, corn and bay leaf; reduce heat and simmer just until potatoes are tender, about 8 minutes. Stir in sugar, basil and oregano; simmer for 20 minutes.

Remove and discard bay leaf. Stir in cream; cook chowder until heated (do not let boil).

In bowl, stir together oil, paprika, garlic, salt and pepper. Add prawns; lightly toss to coat. In skillet, over medium-high heat, sauté prawns until cooked, about 3 minutes per side. Evenly divide chowder among 6 serving bowls; add prawns to each, then sprinkle with green onion.

Serves 6.

Cooking tip
You'll find smoked paprika, a product of Spain, in the spice section of most supermarkets.

South Shore

GALLEY CHOWDER

THE GALLEY RESTAURANT & LOUNGE, CHESTER, NS

This special chowder features local haddock or halibut, shrimp, scallops and lobster. Those ingredients are what visitors and locals alike expect in Nova Scotia chowders and this one delivers in fine style.

1 tablespoon vegetable oil

3 slices bacon, diced

2 celery stalks, finely diced

2 potatoes, diced

1 large white onion, diced

1 carrot, finely diced

1 leek (white and light green parts only), thinly sliced

1 clove garlic, minced

2 tablespoons butter

3 tablespoons all-purpose flour

3 cups warmed fish stock

¾ cup white wine

1 pound haddock or halibut, cut in ¾-inch cubes

8 ounces scallops, halved

8 ounces shrimp, peeled and deveined

6 ounces claw and knuckle lobster meat

1 cup heavy cream (35% m.f.)

⅓ cup finely chopped parsley

1 tablespoon finely chopped fresh rosemary

Salt and pepper to taste

Green onion garnish

In large heavy based saucepan over low heat, warm oil; add bacon and sauté for 3 to 4 minutes. Increase heat to medium and stir in celery, potatoes, onion and carrot; sauté for 3 to 4 minutes. Stir in garlic; sauté for 2 minutes.

Reduce heat to low; stir in butter until melted. Stir in flour until combined; cook for 1 minute. Increase heat to medium and add fish stock and wine; bring to a boil, stirring constantly. Reduce heat and simmer, uncovered, just until vegetables are tender, 8 to 10 minutes.

Increase heat to medium and gently stir in haddock or halibut; cook, stirring often, for 3 minutes.

Gently stir in scallops, shrimp, lobster meat, cream, parsley and rosemary; cook until scallops and shrimp are tender, and heated through, about 4 minutes (do not let boil). Season to taste with salt and pepper. Garnish with green onions.

Serves 6.

📍 Cooking tip
To make curly green onion garnish: slice the white and tender green part of 4 green onions in long very thin strips. Submerge strips in a bowl of ice water and reserve until needed. The strips will curl and form a beautiful garnish.

LUNENBURG SEAFOOD CHOWDER

TRELLIS CAFE,
HUBBARDS, NS

The chefs at Trellis Cafe prepare their chowder base ahead, then add seafood later, in a "fresh to order" approach. This ensures a creamy chowder with seafood that is cooked to perfection.

2 tablespoons butter
1 small onion, finely chopped
1 stalk celery including leaves, chopped
3 potatoes, cubed
6 ounces haddock fillet, cubed
6 ounces scallops
3 ounces shrimp, peeled and deveined
1 cup coffee cream (18% m.f.)
Salt and pepper to taste
2 to 3 cooked lobster claws
Sprigs parsley

In large saucepan over low heat, melt butter; sweat onion and celery until translucent, 10 to 12 minutes. Stir in potatoes and enough water to cover and bring to a boil; cook until potatoes are tender, about 5 minutes.

Gently stir in haddock, scallops and shrimp; simmer until cooked through, 4 to 5 minutes. Gently stir in cream; cook until heated. Season to taste with salt and pepper. Garnish each serving with lobster claw and parsley sprig.

Serves 2 to 3.

Cooking tip
If you opt to add a lighter cream, shred one of the potatoes into the soup base to thicken it.

WHITE POINT'S SMOKED HADDOCK CHOWDER

WHITE POINT BEACH RESORT, HUNTS POINT, NS

After a fire razed the main lodge in 2011, the staff's thoughts were fixated on smoke, so it's somehow appropriate that this chowder uses smoked haddock in cream, coupled with the intense flavour of double-smoked bacon. It's a great way to enjoy leftover planked salmon — a specialty at the lodge — but the chef says you can use any other fish if you prefer.

3 ounces double-smoked bacon, diced
½ cup finely diced onion
½ cup finely diced fennel bulb
2 tablespoons all-purpose flour
½ teaspoon dried thyme
½ teaspoon pepper
8 ounces smoked haddock, cut in bite-size pieces
4 cups half-and-half cream (10% m.f.)
1 ½ cups cubed cooked potatoes
½ pound cooked salmon, cut in bite-size pieces
¼ cup chopped fennel fronds
¾ to 1 teaspoon Montreal Steak Spice
Salt to taste

In saucepan over medium heat, combine bacon, onion and fennel bulb; sauté until bacon is crisp and vegetables are tender, about 8 minutes. Stir in flour, thyme and pepper; cook for 1 minute.

In separate saucepan, combine haddock and cream and bring to a gentle simmer; remove from heat. Stir ½ cup into bacon mixture until blended and smooth. Stir in 1 cup of the cream mixture and bring to a boil, reduce heat to low and simmer until thickened. Stir in remaining cream mixture, potatoes, salmon and fennel fronds; cook until heated through. Stir in Montreal Steak Spice and salt, to taste.

Serves 4 to 6.

DESBARRES MANOR INN SEAFOOD CHOWDER

DESBARRES MANOR INN, GUYSBOROUGH, NS

Blessed is the chef who has an abundant supply of fresh Atlantic seafood at her fingertips. The DesBarres Manor Inn nestles into the shore of Chedabucto Bay — the largest bay on Nova Scotia's Atlantic coast — so the chef can cook up a chowder that's succulent with local lobster, scallops, shrimp, salmon and haddock.

1 onion, finely chopped

1 ¼ pounds unpeeled baby red potatoes, cut in chunks

½ teaspoon sea salt

¼ teaspoon pepper

¾ pound haddock, deboned and cut in bite-size pieces

¼ pound salmon, deboned and cut in bite-size pieces

½ pound sea scallops, connecting muscles removed

¼ pound Atlantic cold-water shrimp, shelled and deveined

¼ pound cooked lobster meat, cut in bite-size pieces

2 cups heavy cream (35% m.f.)

2 cups whole milk (3.5% m.f.)

1 to 2 tablespoons butter

½ tablespoon chopped parsley

½ teaspoon dried thyme

Salt and pepper to taste

In large heavy pot or Dutch oven, place onion, potatoes, salt and pepper. Add just enough water to cover, and bring to a boil; cook just until tender, about 5 minutes. Gently stir in haddock and salmon; return to a boil. Reduce heat to low; simmer until fish flakes easily with fork, about 5 minutes. Gently stir in scallops and shrimp; simmer for 2 minutes. Gently stir in lobster, cream, milk, butter, parsley and thyme; cook until heated through (do not let boil). Season to taste with salt and pepper.

Serves 4 to 6.

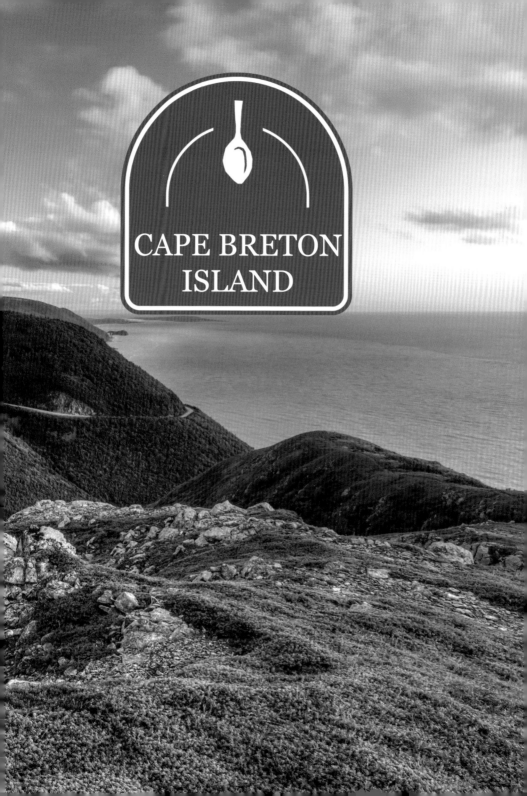

CAPE BRETON
ISLAND

CAPE BRETON SEAFOOD CHOWDER

PANORAMA AT CABOT LINKS, INVERNESS, NS

The folks at Cabot Links believe that almost nothing says "Cape Breton" better than a bowl of steaming seafood chowder. And their version — brimming with lobster, scallops and North Atlantic haddock — is something to talk about. It's won several awards and has been featured in Golf Canada Magazine.

3 to 4 slices bacon
1 potato, cubed
1 leek (white part only), diced
1 carrot, diced
1 celery stalk, diced
¼ pound scallops, halved or quartered if large
1 ¼ cups coffee cream (18% m.f.)
½ pound haddock, cut in chunks
3 ounces lobster meat, cut in bite-size pieces
Salt and pepper to taste
Chopped chives

In skillet, cook bacon until crisp. Let cool, dice and set aside.

In saucepan, combine potato, leek, carrot and celery; add enough water to cover and bring to a boil. Reduce heat and simmer just until vegetables are tender, about 8 minutes. Stir in scallops; simmer for 3 to 4 minutes. Gently stir in cream, haddock, lobster and reserved bacon; cook until seafood is cooked and heated through (do not let boil). Season to taste with salt and pepper. Sprinkle each serving with chives.

Serves 4 to 6.

GOVERNORS SEAFOOD CHOWDER

GOVERNORS PUB & EATERY,
SYDNEY, NS

Filled with fresh Atlantic seafood, this dish will please all ardent chowder lovers. Chef Mofford says that you can replace the heavy cream with Carnation Evaporated Milk. Almost a tradition in the Maritimes, Carnation was commonly used by home cooks as a cream base for chowder. It's lighter but flavourful.

3 potatoes, cubed
2 slices bacon, chopped
1 leek (white part only), thinly sliced
1 onion, finely diced
1 stalk celery, diced
1 tablespoon butter
1 clove garlic, minced
2 tablespoons all-purpose flour
4 cups seafood stock
1 bay leaf
1 sprig each fresh thyme and oregano
½ pound each halibut, redfish and salmon, cubed
½ pound fresh shrimp
½ pound claw and knuckle lobster meat, cut in bite-sized pieces
1 cup heavy cream (35% m.f.)
¼ teaspoon hot sauce
¼ teaspoon Worcestershire sauce
1 teaspoon Old Bay Seasoning (optional)
Salt and white pepper to taste

In large pot of boiling salted water, cook potatoes just until tender. Drain and set aside.

In large saucepan over medium heat, cook bacon until crisp. Reduce heat to low, stir in leek, onion, celery and butter; sweat until vegetables are tender, about 10 minutes. Increase heat to medium; stir in garlic and cook for 1 minute. Stir in flour; cook, stirring constantly, for 2 minutes.

Add seafood stock, bay leaf, thyme and oregano; bring to a simmer and cook for 10 minutes. Stir in reserved potatoes, halibut, redfish, salmon and shrimp; simmer until shrimp are cooked and fish flakes easily with fork, about 5 minutes. Remove and discard bay leaf and sprigs of thyme and oregano; gently stir lobster meat into chowder.

In a small saucepan over medium heat, cook cream until bubbles form around edge; gently stir into chowder and cook until heated through. Stir in hot sauce, Worcestershire sauce, and, if desired, Old Bay Seasoning. Season to taste with salt and pepper.

Serves 6.

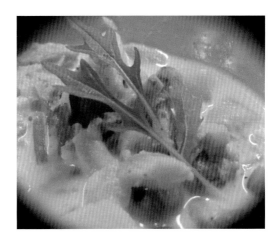

KELTIC LODGE CHOWDER

KELTIC LODGE AND RESORT, INGONISH BEACH, NS

Everything about Keltic Lodge is spectacular and this chowder, full of fresh Atlantic seafood, is a meal in a bowl!

1 cup butter at room temperature, divided
½ cup all-purpose flour
1 medium onion, diced
2 stalks celery, diced
¼ pound mushrooms, sliced
1 cup white wine
8 cups fish stock or water
½ pound salmon, cubed
½ pound haddock, cubed
½ pound scallops
2 cups heavy cream (35% m.f.)
2 (10 ounce) cans baby clams, with juice
½ pound cooked Atlantic cold water shrimp
Salt and pepper to taste

In a small bowl with fingers, blend ½ cup butter with flour, then press into 1-inch balls of roux. Set aside.

In a large saucepan over medium heat melt remaining butter and cook onion, celery and mushrooms until soft, about 5 minutes. Remove vegetables and set aside. Add wine to saucepan and simmer 5 minutes. Stir in fish stock or water, bring to a boil. Gently immerse salmon, haddock and scallops in water and poach until barely cooked, about 2 to 3 minutes. Using a slotted spoon, remove seafood and set aside.

Over high heat reduce stock by a third, about 15 minutes. Whisk roux balls to boiling stock, one at a time, until broth reaches desired consistency.

Add clams with juice and heavy cream. Gently stir in reserved vegetables, seafood and shrimp; return to a simmer. Adjust seasoning with salt and pepper and serve in warmed bowls.

Serves 6 to 8.

YARMOUTH AND
ACADIAN SHORE

HADDOCK CHOWDER

TROUT POINT LODGE,
EAST KEMPTVILLE, NS

"Smooth and subtle" best describes this variation on the traditional Maritime fish chowder. The sage infuses this soup with an aromatic flavour that perfectly complements fresh Atlantic haddock.

2 tablespoons butter

1 tablespoon coarsely chopped fresh sage leaves

1 tablespoon all-purpose flour (preferably organic, non-enriched)

1 onion, coarsely chopped

1 stalk celery, coarsely chopped

3 cups fish stock

1 sweet red pepper, coarsely chopped

1 large potato, cubed

3 cups heavy cream (35% m.f.)

2 pounds haddock, cut in bite-size pieces

1 tablespoon Thai fish sauce

½ teaspoon each salt and pepper

Radish or mustard blossoms (optional)

In stockpot or large saucepan over medium-low heat, melt butter; sauté sage just until golden and fragrant. Stir in flour until blended and smooth. Stir in onion and celery; sauté for 3 minutes. Stir in fish stock; cook until vegetables are tender, about 10 minutes. Remove from heat and let cool slightly. Transfer to blender; purée until smooth.

Return to stockpot over low heat and stir in red pepper, potato and cream; bring to a simmer and cook until potatoes are almost tender, about 7 minutes.

Gently stir in haddock, fish sauce, salt and pepper; cook until heated through, about 5 minutes (do not let boil). Adjust seasoning, if desired. Garnish each serving with radish blossoms, if desired.

Serves 6.

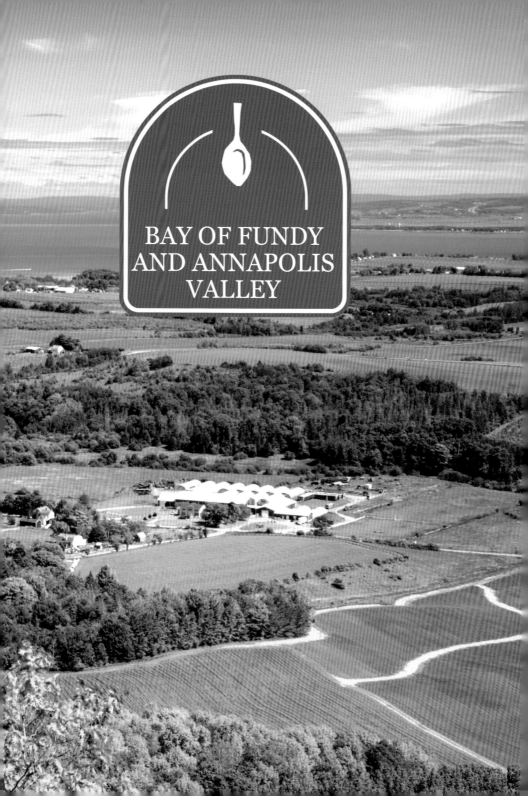

BAY OF FUNDY
AND ANNAPOLIS
VALLEY

DIGBY PINES SMOKED HADDOCK AND BACON CHOWDER WITH THYME

DIGBY PINES GOLF RESORT AND SPA, DIGBY, NS

As Dale Nichols began his career at the Pines, he learned that locally smoked haddock was available. Taking a gamble, he replaced the traditional Acadian seafood chowder listed on the menu with this smoked haddock recipe. Now nobody asks for the old stuff anymore.

½ pound bacon, cut in bite-size pieces
3 potatoes, cubed
¼ cup butter
2 small celery stalks, finely diced
1 onion, finely diced
1 tablespoon fresh thyme leaves (1 teaspoon dried)
1 pound smoked haddock, cubed
3 to 4 tablespoons rice flour
2 cups fish stock
1 cup heavy cream (35% m.f.)
½ cup milk (2% m.f.)
Salt and pepper to taste

In skillet, sauté bacon until almost crisp; with slotted spoon, transfer to paper towel to drain, set aside.

In large pot of boiling salted water, cook potatoes until tender; drain and set aside.

In large saucepan over medium-high heat, melt butter; sauté celery, onion and thyme until onion is translucent, about 5 minutes. Gently stir in reserved bacon and haddock; sprinkle with flour and stir to combine.

Stir in fish stock; cook, stirring, until mixture begins to thicken. Stir in reserved potatoes, cream and milk, reduce heat and bring to a simmer; cook for 5 minutes. Season to taste with salt and pepper.

Serves 4 to 6.

MUSSEL AND GRILLED CORN CHOWDER

FRONT & CENTRAL RESTAURANT, WOLFVILLE, NS

Originally developed as a play on classic vichyssoise, this offers an interesting spin on classic chowder and features fresh, in-season corn and locally farmed mussels. A garnish of camelina oil lends a beautiful pea flavour, and smoked paprika echoes the subtle smoke of the mussels. Served chilled, it's ideal for summer, but it's equally delicious served warm on cooler days.

1 tablespoon canola oil, divided
Corn sliced from 4 cobs, divided
Salt and pepper to taste
2 pounds mussels
Alder, apple, oak or pecan wood chips
2 tablespoons butter
1 leek (white part only), thinly sliced
2 cups diced celery root
1 cup diced fennel bulb
½ cup sliced shallots
½ cup white wine
2 cups fish stock
1 cup chicken stock

1 cup heavy cream (35% m.f.)
1 cup cubed Yukon gold potato
3 sprigs fresh thyme
1 bay leaf
Zest of 1 lemon
1 stalk lemongrass, trimmed, bruised
   and cut in 1-inch pieces
2 tablespoons sliced fresh ginger
Tabasco sauce to taste
Smoked paprika to taste
Camelina oil to taste
Fresh pea shoots

Set barbeque on high. With small amount of the oil, rub 2 cobs of the corn, then season to taste with salt and pepper. Grill, turning with tongs, until kernels are tender and marked. Remove from grill and let cool enough to handle; slice kernels from cobs and set aside.

From remaining cobs, slice kernels; transfer to blender and purée, adding small amount of water if necessary to achieve a smooth consistency. Through fine-mesh sieve, strain into bowl, pressing solids to extract liquid. Discard solids and set corn purée aside.

Under cold running water, scrub and de-beard mussels, discarding any that are damaged or don't close when lightly tapped. Evenly arrange mussels in a single layer in disposable foil pan.

In another disposable foil pan, spread even layer of wood chips; sprinkle with water. Grill until smoking, 2 to 8 minutes. Transfer mussel pan to grill alongside wood-chip pan; close lid and smoke for 10 minutes. At halfway point quickly lift lid and stir mussels. (If mussels remain unopened, smoke for 2 to 3 minutes more.) Reserving cooking liquid and discarding any unopened mussels, transfer mussels to bowl with tongs and set aside. Strain cooking liquid through fine-mesh sieve into separate bowl; set aside.

In large saucepan over medium heat, warm butter and remaining oil; sauté leek, celery root, fennel bulb and shallots until softened, 6 to 8 minutes.

Increase heat to high and add wine; cook, stirring to deglaze pan, until most of the liquid has evaporated. Stir in fish stock, chicken stock, cream, potato, reserved corn purée, thyme and bay leaf; bring to a boil. Reduce heat to low; cook, stirring occasionally, until potato and celery root are tender, about 8 minutes. Remove from heat. Remove and discard thyme and bay leaf. Stir in lemon zest.

Transfer to blender; in batches, purée until smooth. Return to pan over low heat; stir in lemongrass and ginger and simmer for 10 minutes. With slotted spoon, remove and discard lemongrass and ginger. Stir in reserved mussel-cooking liquid. Season broth to taste with salt and Tabasco.

To serve warm: Stir in reserved corn and mussels; cook until heated through. To serve cold: Transfer broth to airtight container and refrigerate until chilled. Evenly divide reserved corn between serving bowls. Ladle chilled broth overtop, then arrange reserved mussels around corn.

Garnish with a dash of paprika, drizzled camelina oil and topping of fresh pea shoots.

Serves 6 to 8.

SPANISH CHOWDER

LE CAVEAU RESTAURANT, DOMAINE DE GRAND PRÉ, GRAND PRÉ, NS

Chef Jason Lynch says, "This chowder was influenced by a trip to Spain, when I had Ajo Blanco, a white gazpacho, and thought that — with a little tweak — it would pair beautifully with scallops and lobster."

4 slices potato or rustic bread, crusts removed and torn in pieces
½ cup heavy cream (35% m.f.)
3 cups water
1 cup chicken stock
2 cloves garlic, finely minced
4 tablespoons ground blanched almonds
Sea salt and white pepper
8 scallops, halved
8 ounces lobster meat, cut in bite-size pieces
Toasted slivered almonds
Green onions, thinly sliced
Pinch of smoked paprika

In bowl, combine bread and cream; let soak for 20 minutes.

In large saucepan, combine water and stock; bring to a boil. Reduce heat to low; stir in bread mixture, garlic and blanched almonds. Remove from heat; with immersion blender, purée until smooth (or transfer to blender; purée until smooth, then return to pan).

Return to heat and season to taste with salt and white pepper; bring to a simmer. Gently stir in scallops; cook for 2 minutes.

Evenly divide lobster meat between serving bowls; ladle chowder overtop. Sprinkle with slivered almonds, green onions and paprika.

Serves 4.

MASSTOWN MARKET'S FAMOUS SEAFOOD CHOWDER

MASSTOWN MARKET, MASSTOWN, NS

Inspired by the nearby Bay of Fundy, the chowder recipe from Masstown Market has evolved into a heaping bowl of fresh seafood in a rich, savory broth. At the market, the chowder is served with warm biscuits topped with creamery butter.

3 tablespoons unsalted butter
1 large onion, diced
3 celery stalks, chopped
4 cups cubed potatoes
4 cups water
1 bay leaf
¼ onion
½ pound haddock fillet, cubed
½ pound cod filet, cubed
½ pound scallops, halved if large
⅓ cup unsalted butter
⅓ cup all-purpose flour
4 ounces cooked lobster, cut in bite-size pieces
4 ounces Atlantic cold-water shrimp
2 cups half-and-half cream (10% m.f.) or coffee cream (18% m.f.)
Pinch nutmeg
Salt and pepper to taste
Chopped parsley, as garnish (optional)

In large heavy saucepan or Dutch oven over medium heat, melt butter; sauté diced onion until translucent, about 3 minutes. Stir in celery; sauté for 10 minutes. Stir in potatoes and add just enough water to cover; bring to a boil. Reduce heat to low; cook until potatoes are tender. Drain and set aside.

In another saucepan over medium heat, combine water, bay leaf and quarter onion; bring almost to a boil. Maintaining just below boil, gently stir in haddock, cod and scallops; poach until fish flakes easily with fork and scallops are opaque, about 5 minutes. With slotted spoon, transfer solids to bowl. Remove and discard bay leaf and onion. Set solids and poaching liquid aside.

In another saucepan over medium heat, melt butter; whisk in flour and cook, whisking constantly, for 1 minute. Slowly whisk in reserved poaching liquid; cook until smooth and thickened into sauce. Stir in reserved onion and haddock mixtures, lobster and shrimp. Gently stir in cream; cook until heated through. Season to taste with nutmeg, salt and pepper. Garnish with chopped parsley if desired.

Serves 6 to 8.

CHIPOTLE MUSSEL CHOWDER

OLD ORCHARD INN, GREENWICH, NS

Hot chipotle pepper gives this rosy coloured mussel chowder its bite. Adjust the heat by increasing or decreasing the amount of pepper.

2 pounds mussels
½ cup white wine
1 tablespoon minced garlic
6 whole peppercorns
2 cups cubed potatoes
1 tablespoon olive oil
2 stalks celery, diced
½ cup chopped onion
2 tomatoes, diced (or one 14.5-ounce can diced tomatoes, with juice
½ to 1 chipotle pepper in adobo sauce
1 cup heavy cream (35% m.f.)
Salt and pepper to taste

Under cold running water, scrub and de-beard mussels, discarding any that are damaged or don't close when lightly tapped. Set aside.

In large saucepan, combine wine, garlic and peppercorns; bring to a boil. Stir in mussels; cover and cook until mussels have opened, about 5 minutes. Reserving cooking liquid, drain. Remove and discard any unopened mussels; set aside until cool enough to handle. Remove mussel meat from shells and set aside; discard shells.

In large pot of boiling salted water, cook potatoes just until tender; drain and set aside.

In large saucepan over medium-low heat, heat oil; sauté celery and onion until tender, about 8 minutes. Stir in tomatoes, reserved potatoes, chipotle pepper and reserved cooking liquid; bring to a simmer.

Stir in cream and reserved mussel meat; cook until heated through. Season to taste with salt and pepper.

Serves 4 to 6.

Cooking tip

Chipotle peppers in adobo sauce can be found in the Mexican specialty section of most supermarkets. You can transfer leftover peppers to an airtight container and freeze them for future use.

NORTHUMBERLAND
SHORE

CHEF GABRIEAU'S SEAFOOD CHOWDER

GABRIEAU'S BISTRO, ANTIGONISH, NS

Chef Gabrieau tells the story of this chowder: The naturally sweet parsnip was added at the suggestion of a woman in one of his early cooking classes, while the sautéed bacon (often used in Atlantic Canadian chowders) was left out to accommodate vegetarians who consume seafood but not meat. A popular recipe, this won the historic Sherbrooke Village seafood-chowder contest three years running.

2 ½ cups cubed potatoes
½ cup diced parsnip
¼ cup butter
1 bay leaf
1 cup chopped sweet onion
1 cup finely diced celery
½ cup finely diced carrot
1 ½ teaspoon minced garlic
½ teaspoon dried thyme
½ cup dry white wine
1 pound haddock, cut in chunks
4 ounces salmon, cut in chunks
4 cups half-and-half cream (10% m.f.)
½ cup each chopped lobster meat, small shrimp, chopped mock crab, sliced scallops
1 can (10 ounce) baby clams, with juice

Salt and pepper to taste
1 to 2 teaspoons fish-base seasoning (optional)
Chopped parsley or fresh chives or dill

In large pot of boiling salted water, cook potatoes and parsnip just until tender, about 10 minutes. Set aside (do not drain).

In large saucepan over medium-low heat, melt butter; sweat bay leaf, onion, celery, carrot, garlic and thyme until vegetables are tender, 10 to 12 minutes. Increase heat to high and add wine; cook, stirring to deglaze pan for about 1 minute.

Stir in reserved potatoes, parsnip and cooking liquid; bring to a simmer. Gently stir in haddock and salmon; simmer until fish flakes easily with fork, about 5 minutes.

In large heavy saucepan over medium heat, warm cream until bubbles begin to form around edge; pour into broth. Gently stir in lobster meat, shrimp, mock crab, scallops and clams with juice; simmer for 10 minutes (do not let boil). Season to taste with salt and pepper, adding fish-base seasoning, if desired. Sprinkle each serving with parsley.

Serves 4 to 6.

PICTOU LODGE CHOWDER

PICTOU LODGE BEACH RESORT, PICTOU, NS

Diners at Pictou Lodge who order seafood chowder are served steaming bowls of soup accompanied by Buttermilk Tea Biscuits slathered in Molasses Butter. Luckily for us, the chef also shared his biscuit and butter recipes (page 87). To make this chowder easier to prepare, home cooks can use three cups of water and three teaspoons of fish-base seasoning, instead of making homemade stock.

½ pound mussels
2 potatoes, cubed
1 carrot, diced
½ cup butter
1 stalk celery, chopped
¼ large onion, diced
⅓ cup all-purpose flour
3 cups Fish Stock (recipe follows)
2 cups heavy cream (35% m.f.)
¾ cup white wine
1 ¼ pounds mixed seafood such as clams, haddock, scallops, salmon
Pinch nutmeg
Pinch cayenne pepper
Salt and pepper to taste
2 tablespoons chopped fresh dill

Under cold running water, scrub and de-beard mussels, discarding any that are damaged or don't close when lightly tapped. Set aside.

In large pot of boiling salted water, cook potatoes and carrot until tender, about 10 minutes. Drain and set aside.

In large saucepan over medium-high heat, melt butter; sauté celery and onion until translucent, about 5 minutes. Sprinkle with flour and cook, stirring constantly, for 2 minutes. Whisk in fish stock, cream and wine; reduce heat to bring to a simmer and cook until thickened and smooth (do not let boil).

Gently stir in mixed seafood and reserved mussels; cover and simmer until fish flakes easily with fork and mussels have opened, about 5 minutes. Remove and discard any unopened mussels. Gently stir in reserved potato mixture; cook until heated through. Stir in nutmeg and cayenne. Season to taste with salt and pepper to taste. Sprinkle each serving with dill. Serve with Pictou Lodge's Buttermilk Tea Biscuits and Molasses Butter (page 87)

Serves 4 to 6.

FISH STOCK

For this delicate stock, use lean, white-fleshed fish such as cod, haddock, halibut, pollock or ocean perch (high-fat species have too strong a flavour).

2 pounds fish trimmings, with bones
2 celery stalks, chopped
2 bay leaves
1 onion, quartered
1 tablespoon whole peppercorns

Rinse fish bones. In stockpot, combine bones and enough cold water to cover; bring to a boil. Reduce heat and simmer, skimming off foam that rises to surface. Stir in celery, bay leaves, onion and peppercorns. Simmer for 45 minutes. Through fine-mesh sieve lined with cheesecloth, strain into bowl.

Yields 3 to 4 cups.

Cooking tip
To store this stock, transfer to airtight container; refrigerate for up to 3 days or freeze for up to 3 months.

BISCUITS AND ACCOMPANIMENTS

CHIVES BUTTERMILK BISCUITS

CHIVES CANADIAN BISTRO,
HALIFAX, NS

These "drop" biscuits are quicker to prepare than the rolled-and-cut variety — and their irregular edges brown and crisp while they bake, giving them a lovely texture. Chef Craig Flinn says that Chives has served these same biscuits every night since it opened.

4 cups unbleached white flour
4 teaspoons baking powder
4 teaspoons granulated sugar
½ teaspoon salt
½ pound butter, cubed
3 eggs
1 ½ cups buttermilk

In large bowl, whisk together flour, baking powder, sugar and salt; with pastry blender or 2 knives, cut in butter until texture resembles coarse meal.

In another bowl, beat eggs with buttermilk. Slowly add flour mixture, running fork down side of bowl to centre and back up, turning bowl as you work, until dough forms.

With large spoon, drop 2 ½-inch balls of dough onto nonstick baking pan. Bake in centre of 400°F oven until golden, 12 to 15 minutes. Serve warm.

Makes 18 to 20 biscuits.

BUTTERMILK TEA BISCUITS

PICTOU LODGE BEACH RESORT, PICTOU, NS

At Pictou Lodge, the chowder is always served with these buttermilk tea biscuits and the dark and decadent Molasses Butter.

1 ¾ cups all-purpose flour
1 tablespoon baking powder
5 teaspoons granulated sugar
1 teaspoon salt
⅓ cup butter, cubed
2 large eggs, divided
1 cup buttermilk
2 tablespoons milk

In bowl, whisk together flour, baking powder, sugar and salt; with pastry blender or 2 knives, cut in butter until mixture resembles fine crumbs.

In small bowl, whisk 1 of the eggs with buttermilk; with fork, stir into flour mixture until dough forms. On lightly floured surface, gently knead 4 or 5 times. Roll out, cut with round biscuit cutter; transfer to parchment paper-lined baking sheet.

In another small bowl, whisk remaining egg and milk; brush over biscuits. Bake in centre of 400°F oven until golden, 12 to 15 minutes. Serve warm with Molasses Butter.

Makes 8 to 10 biscuits.

MOLASSES BUTTER

¼ pound butter, softened
¾ cup light or low sugar molasses

In small bowl, beat butter until light and fluffy, about 5 minutes. Beat in molasses until blended and smooth. Cover and refrigerate until serving.

Makes 1 cup.

CABOT LINKS CHIVE BISCUITS

PANORAMA AT CABOT LINKS, INVERNESS, NS

Sharpened up with the fresh bite of chives, these tasty little biscuits are perfect beside a steaming bowl of chowder.

2 ½ cups all-purpose flour
⅓ cup granulated sugar
¼ cup chopped fresh chives
1 tablespoon baking powder
⅓ cup butter, softened
3 eggs, divided
1 ¼ cups milk

In bowl, whisk together flour, sugar, chives and baking powder; with pastry blender or 2 knives, cut in butter until mixture resembles fine crumbs. Form a well in centre.

In another bowl, whisk 2 of the eggs with milk; pour into well in flour mixture and stir until dough forms. With large spoon, drop balls of dough onto nonstick or parchment paper-lined baking sheet.

In small bowl, whisk remaining egg (or yolk or white only) with small amount of water; brush over biscuits. Bake in centre of 400°F oven until slightly golden, about 12 minutes.

Makes 12 biscuits.

JOHNNYCAKE

There are probably as many renditions of johnnycake as there are cookbooks — ranging from flat cornmeal pancakes to leavened breads served warm in squares. This one's dense and just the thing to serve with lighter chowders.

2 cups all-purpose flour
1 cup cornmeal
$\frac{1}{2}$ cup granulated sugar
5 teaspoons baking powder
$\frac{1}{2}$ teaspoon baking soda
$\frac{1}{2}$ teaspoon salt
2 eggs, beaten
1 $\frac{1}{2}$ cups milk
$\frac{1}{2}$ cup molasses
$\frac{1}{2}$ cup butter, melted

In large bowl, whisk together flour, cornmeal, sugar, baking powder, baking soda and salt.

   In another large bowl, stir together eggs, milk, molasses and melted butter. A little at a time, stir in flour mixture until combined. Scrape into greased 9 x 12-inch baking pan; bake in centre of 350°F oven until cake tester inserted in centre comes out clean, 50 to 55 minutes. Cut into squares; serve warm.

Serves 6 to 8.

INDEX

PHOTO CREDITS

Unless otherwise specified, photography was supplied by the various establishments and properties and by Taste of NS. The exceptions are: istockphoto pages 3, 8-9, 11, 24-25, 50-51, 54-55, 62-63, 66-67, 77, 78-79, 84-85.